A STEP BY STEP BOOK ABOUT
CHINCHILLAS

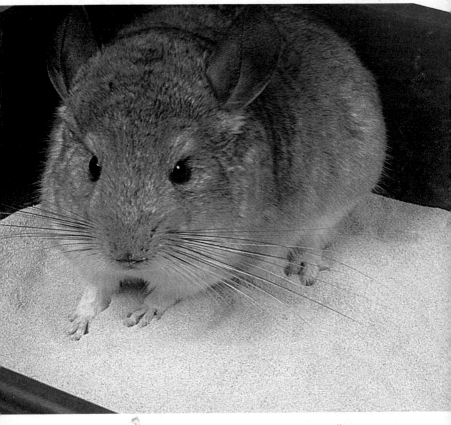

HORST KÜHNER

Photography:
Dr. Herbert R. Axelrod, Isabelle Francais, Michael Gilroy, John Zeinert.

Humorous illustrations by Andrew Prendimano.

TRANSLATED BY HOWARD H. HIRSCHHORN.

Distributed in the UNITED STATES by T.F.H. Publications, Inc., 211 West Sylvania Avenue, Neptune City, NJ 07753; in CANADA to the Book Trade by Macmillan of Canada (A Division of Canada Publishing Corporation), 164 Commander Boulevard, Agincourt, Ontario M1S 3C7; in ENGLAND by T.F.H. Publications Limited, 4 Kier Park, Ascot, Berkshire SL5 7DS; in AUSTRALIA AND THE SOUTH PACIFIC by T.F.H. (Australia) Pty. Ltd., Box 149, Brookvale 2100 N.S.W., Australia; in NEW ZEALAND by Ross Haines & Son, Ltd., 18 Monmouth Street, Grey Lynn, Auckland 2, New Zealand; in SINGAPORE AND MALAYSIA by MPH Distributors (S) Pte., Ltd., 601 Sims Drive, #03/07/21, Singapore 1438; in the PHILIPPINES by Bio-Research, 5 Lippay Street, San Lorenzo Village, Makati Rizal; in SOUTH AFRICA by Multipet Pty. Ltd., 30 Turners Avenue, Durban 4001. Published by T.F.H. Publications, Inc. Manufactured in the United States of America by T.F.H. Publications, Inc.

CONTENTS

PREFACE

The keeping, care, and breeding of small animals has become a necessity these days for many people. They find such activity keeps them somewhat in touch with nature, from which we're all getting further and further away all the time. The exaggerations of technology have so far removed our daily lives from nature that many people can hardly even understand it any more. In many places on earth, people are almost about to destroy the very natural environment in which our grandparents were able to survive. It would be hard to find any way to return to nature, for industrialization has made things so easy and pleasant that we wouldn't want to forgo them. But people still foster their own little ties with nature by keeping and caring for household pets. This shows that, despite technological control of our environment, there is still the desire to remain part of nature.

This is certainly the moving force behind the expansion of the pet industry, whose business is still climbing sharply. More and more pet shops are meeting this need of people for animals. The corner merchant and the gas station operator on the side street would probably like to get even a small slice of this large pie. There is the danger, however, that the whole industry will be accused of living *from* animals instead of *for* them. For that reason, I would ask all readers of this book to please consider carefully where they shop for their pets and where they buy food for them. Thus they can decide where they can expect to find the best professional advice.

FACING PAGE:
Chinchillas should not be kept as pets purely on a whim. Before deciding to obtain a pet chinchilla, a new owner should give careful consideration to how well he can meet the needs of the animal.

A CHINCHILLA STORY

One morning a little girl went into a pet shop and looked around. The clerk was busy, so she had time to study the animals in their cages—rabbits, guinea pigs, hamsters, kangaroo mice (or jerboas), chipmunks—all of which she had seen often and knew well enough. But there was another little animal, about the size of a guinea pig, that she didn't recognize. It immediately caught her interest, and as soon as the clerk had time for her, the following conversation took place.

"You've got a cute little animal in the cage over there, the gray animal with the large button eyes." "That's a chinchilla," the clerk replied, but her answer went over the little girl's head. "It has a bushy tail like a squirrel and large round eyes like Mickey Mouse, so is it a rabbit?" the little girl insisted.

The clerk finally realized that there was real interest here, so she made an effort to give the girl a more detailed answer. "No, that's not a rabbit. Rabbits don't have long bushy tails or round ears. Rabbit ears are long and pointed. This is quite another kind of animal."

"Is it a hamster?"

"No, though its large button-like eyes make it seem familiar to us. Many twilight and nocturnal animals have large dark eyes, which are especially adapted to seeing and getting around in the dark. Although it looks vaguely like a long-tailed golden hamster, it is not closely related to any of our common pet animals. Like the hamsters, mice, and guinea pig, it is a rodent, but it belongs in its own family, Chinchillidae."

"Where does it come from?"

FACING PAGE:
Chinchillas are appealing animals with a distinctive cuddly charm, so it's easy to see why they're rapidly increasing in popularity.

"This one came from a breeder, but the chinchillas' original home is the dry areas of the high Andes and Cordillera in South America, where they are quite well adapted to local conditions."

"Why haven't I ever seen an animal like it before in a pet shop?"

"The breeding of chinchillas was a problem for a long time, so the few animals born in captivity became quite expensive and were available only from breeders. But now the stocks are larger, and the breeding and rearing of the young is much easier because of improved feed. So now their lower price as well as the ability to feed them properly makes them attractive as pets."

"Can you just keep them in a cage?"

"Breeders have accustomed chinchillas to caged life. A large rabbit cage with the usual accessories is suitable."

"Do they have to stay in their cage?"

A caged female chinchilla being tempted with a tidbit. Chinchillas readily adapt to life in properly constructed cages.

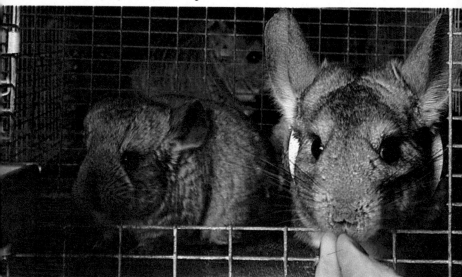

A Chinchilla Story

"Well, they did grow up in cages, but they still are happy at every chance they get to romp around. But watch them carefully if they are allowed to run free around the house because they are rodents and could do some gnawing damage. In general, they're no more dangerous than hares, rabbits, guinea pigs, and hamsters."

"How do you get the chinchillas back into the cage?"

"It's best to let them out only before feeding them; then, while they're still hungry, you can entice them back in

Alert and curious, these young chinchillas show coat colors different from that of the wild chinchilla.

with a tasty morsel of food. If that fails, you can catch them by gripping them at the base of the tail. Grabbing a chinchilla by the fur might rip some hair out of it."

"Are they active only at night?"

"Chinchillas are twilight creatures who see well with their large eyes, so they are mainly up and about at dawn and in the evening. They shy away from harsh light and need a quiet place into which to retreat undisturbed during the day."

This young chinchilla is being safely supported by the hands of its owner, but it's still a little fearful. A greater degree of support would be provided by cradling the animal against the chest.

"How do you feed and take care of chinchillas?"

"You give them a tablespoonful of feed morning and evening, plus an occasional handful of hay. Also, give them fresh water in the drinker once a day, and clean the cage once a week. Besides that, they only need a few kind words and sometimes a tasty snack so they feel comfortable near us."

"Do chinchillas have an odor?"

"They have a very faint one. Their droppings, too, are almost odorless. Chinchillas are the most unobtrusive pets in this respect. Cleaning the cage once a week is quite adequate."

"Should you keep only one as a pet?"

"As a rule you might say yes, because a single animal gets used to human company easier. But if you don't have much time for your pet, then it's better to have a mate for it."

"Which sex makes the best pets?"

"It's best to buy young males. They tame the fastest. Young females can spray quite a lot of urine if they aren't handled right. But with patience this isn't any problem for a skillful handler."

A Chinchilla Story

"How old do chinchillas get to be?"

"On the average about eight to ten years old. My oldest animal, a male named Mohammed, was 13 years old. I'm sure other breeders have even older ones, that is retired ones, of course, who don't breed any more."

"Would you recommend a chinchilla as a pet for me?"

"Yes, chinchillas are very interesting pets. You've shown a lot of interest in this animal and patiently listened to my explanations—both desirable qualifications for being a pet owner. If you have room, then I would certainly entrust you with an animal like this."

Cages for chinchillas are available in different sizes, but all should be equipped with the same basic accessories regardless of size.

CHOOSING YOUR PET

All animal lovers about to acquire a pet should first discover just what kind of pet is best for them. A passing fancy should not be the basis of a decision. It takes serious consideration. Beware of impulse buying! It's a good idea to read a book on the animal you're considering and learn just what a pet really requires of its owner. A book like that will be a good reference for you later on. For people who enjoy having an animal to pet and enjoy the choice is great. "Pettable" animals are the right choice—dogs, cats, rabbits, guinea pigs, hamsters and many other animals. For people who work during the day, and who want a charming, alert animal in the evening when they come home, a chinchilla is a good choice. Our experience has shown that young families, with both spouses working daytime, are interested in these animals. In such households, the home is quiet all day long, and a chinchilla can sleep undisturbed. In the evening, when the pet owners return home, these small fellows are there waiting to say "hello," actively scampering around the cage. It's evening feeding time, and even when there is only a little time to play with your pet, he's happy and content. For the owner, too, an evening like that is very relaxing and lets him forget many of his work-a-day problems.

If you're a person who likes to pet animals and who wants a most satisfying tactile experience then you should pet a chinchilla. The wonderful softness of this fur cannot be described; it must be felt in order to understand why, since its discovery during the Spanish conquest of South America, it was so desired by the few families who could afford it—as a fur

FACING PAGE:
Upper photo: This chinchilla is using its forefeet to raise an object to its mouth for examination. *Lower photo:* Obviously feeling secure in its owner's cupped hands, this chinchilla has begun to explore its surroundings.

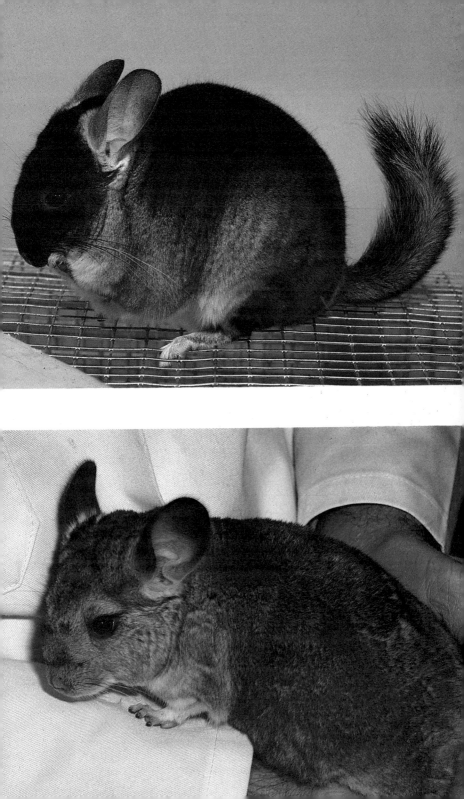

coat. The public at large has become more involved in the expansion of the fur trade since then. Even at the beginning of this century, the dream of chinchilla fur coats was fulfilled for many well-to-do families. Unfortunately, because of this the animal was almost annihilated. Today, however, their number has increased because of breeding farms. The pet industry has gotten involved and is not doing so badly at all. The animals have proven very amenable to the breeding conditions. They were born and reared in cages, so are especially suitable for the pet owner. A little rascal like that certainly brings joy into a home. Owning a chinchilla doesn't have to remain a dream to be fulfilled only for the specialists among pet lovers. These animals are being sold by more and more pet shops, as well as directly by the breeders. Accessories for them are available too.

This little book is meant to provide the theoretical framework for acquiring and maintaining the chinchilla. We've tried to cover all pertinent questions in as much detail as needed to make caring for the chinchilla easy for all pet lovers.

Description of the Best-Known Kinds

Chinchillas are a small genus of the rodent family with a number of known species, all from South America. Some stocks there, however, are extinct or exist only as remnants in natural preserves. The largest of these species was the king or royal chinchilla, but unfortunately there are no more living members left of this most beautiful of all the species.

We know its size from old written records and from furs which were all the rage at the Spanish court at the beginning of the 18th century. Judging from the size of the furs, it must have been a rather large animal. Coloration, fur quality and habits were similar to those of other known species caught during the same epoch. This king chinchilla would have interested fur breeders very much, but perhaps would have been much too large, it must have been about the size of a rabbit.

The two most widespread kinds today are the broad-headed and the pointed-headed chinchillas. These aren't the technical names, but characterize the animals quite well. The broad-headed type, also called the La Plata type, has a short,

broad head with round ears, very solid body build, and thick, somewhat woolly fur of light-to-medium gray color.

The pointed-head type, also called the Costina type, seems much thinner because of its longer ears and stretched body build. Its fur grows more evenly and is medium-to-dark gray, so is of more interest to the fur trade.

Chinchillas being bred today are mainly from crosses of these two types—an effort to combine the good characteristics of both kinds into a new breeding strain. This very complicated breeding seems successful, and the resulting animals stand out from animals still living in the wild. Common to them all is the unusually colored fur, of which each hair has three color gradations. The largest portion of the hair, the lower portion, is usually dark gray. Above it is a narrow, light-colored (or, ideally, white) band. At the tips, the hair becomes dark gray again. This fur is so characteristic that other breeding animals with similar fur coloration are described as "chinchilla color."

Like that of most other animals, the fur of chinchillas also is composed of two different types of hair. The most interesting part is the brush, which gives the fur its thickness and fullness. It consists of a root down in the skin, and up to 60 single hairs coming up out of this root. This brush is so light that it waves in the slightest air movement; that's even lighter than a feather. The caretaker of the animal needs to be especially watchful. Loose hairs have to be balled together with the fingertips and thrown away. The second kind of hair is bristle— much thicker, stiff hairs which give form to the fur and straighten it up, making it resilient. Fur is completely renewed once every year. An animal's first fur grows by 8 to 10 months, and thereafter regrows at intervals of 12 months.

Don't alarm a chinchilla by poking at it through the openings of its cage.

Chinchillas come from South America, where they live in the Cordillera and the Andes, in the caves and rock crevices where they hide from their worst enemies, birds of prey, and protect themselves from the intense sunlight. They range up to the highest levels, even up to the snow line. Cold doesn't faze them, for Nature has provided them with a very thick fur, which protects them from loss of body heat. It's also very loose, and many an attacking condor has seized only a bunch of hair from its intended prey, which scampered away uninjured to its protective cave.

LIFE CYCLE AND CAGING

The humidity in those places is very slight, rarely above 30%. It hardly rains. Any precipitation occurs as snow in the winter. For this reason, chinchillas don't need any oily, water-repellent outer hair. The ground is stony to sandy, and the growing period very short. So chinchillas feed for most of the year on dry berries, roots, dry grasses and bark, which they gnaw from branches. To fully utilize this poor diet, they have a very long intestinal tract which tends to be upset by too rich a diet. Their care requires watchfulness for ballast or roughage, which can be added to their feed in the form of hay, dry fruit and twigs. Because chinchillas are from regions with scant water, yet spend so much time grooming their fur, we can expect once again to find something quite special here and we do! They bathe in dry rocky dust, powder themselves thoroughly with it, then shake it off along with the greasy skin and fur debris which sticks to it. And that's how they get their clean, fragrant fur. In captivity, a sand bath replaces the natural mineral dust.

FACING PAGE:
The beautiful thick, plush fur of the chinchilla will be at its best only if the animal is fed properly and given good care.

These very particular habits have to be kept in mind when dealing with a captive chinchilla or determining whether one condition or another is useful or harmful. You must try to understand this animal, who was brought from a completely different habitat into our own world and is hard put to stay healthy, active, and also still reproduce regularly and vigorously. A real pet lover, however, will not find it hard to understand his animal. Their behavior reveals their mood immediately. An animal which at the slightest sound comes to the wire or screening and waits for a word from its owner is in very good condition. Sickly animals flee from people and try to deal with their misery alone in a corner of the cage.

Visit a chinchilla breeder one evening at mealtime and see all the activity, and hear the sounds the animals make as they jump around, eat, bathe, and quarrel among themselves. You'll immediately recognize its voice as it expresses itself: a short, sharp bleating when a female doesn't want to let her mate get to the feed pan yet; a faint peeping of the babies who couldn't keep up fast enough with their mother on the way to the food; a soft purring when feeding is over and the animals are resting again at their places; the combative bleating and whistling when two males tangle at a territorial border, or when a female won't allow another to approach her brood. Every pet owner should become familiar with these various sounds so as to understand his animals. It's important, too, to maintain vocal contact with your chinchillas. Every pet owner

Two young chinchillas showing the same intent curiosity as their alert mother.

should say a few words every time he comes near his animal. That calms it more than you can imagine. Even while you're cleaning the cage, don't neglect this "conversation." The chinchilla is certainly not overjoyed when major housecleaning hits his territory every week. So to keep your pet from taking it all too badly, you've got to soothe it with few kind words.

A pet owner has to help his pet feel at home. Only then can its care be called optimal. The chinchilla has to become part of the family, just as in the wild it grows up with its chinchilla family and finds its niche in life. A chinchilla with "family connections" always feels comfortable in his foster home and doesn't need anything special, except your remembering not to let your pet roam around the house without su-

These chinchillas have been provided with fruit tree branches and wooden blocks to gnaw on. Never give chinchillas wood that has been treated with chemical preservatives to keep it from rotting.

pervision. When you're busy, it belongs in its cage. This isn't just because the chinchilla as a rodent likes to munch on a chair leg or corner of another piece of furniture. It's because chinchillas can hurt themselves on such an excursion; they might eat something they can't digest or even become fatalities.

A few examples will illustrate the great danger for our pets. One summer a family went out into the garden, and their chinchilla jumped up on the windowsill in an effort to get through the window and follow along. They called out to it and started back to the house to put their pet back into its cage, but it sprang through the opened window and died from injuries suffered after its fall from the second floor.

There's another story. Tame "Chinchi" had the run of the hallway for half a year and had already partially nibbled away the bathroom wallpaper. New wallpaper was to be put up. First came the hallway, so Chinchi was locked up in the bathroom. For the evening, the paperhanger's bucket with the rest of the wallpaper paste was put in the bathroom for use again the next morning—and that cost the family pet its life because, as was to be expected from its curiosity, it stuck its nose somewhat too deeply into the bucket. And that should be enough of stories. Heed this urgent advice, however, and let chinchillas loose only under supervision. Chinchillas are, above all, twilight and nocturnal animals. Their large eyes and long whiskers are unmistakable signs of dim-light specialists. They live in family units and communicate by means of soft bleating. When danger threatens, however, they can emit loud warning calls which send the whole family scurrying for cover. If they are cornered by an enemy, they stand up and in some cases spray urine. This behavior is also a problem at first for an inexperienced keeper or pet owner. A tamed chinchilla, however, soon abandons this habit.

If we consider the habitat to which these animals have adapted, there seem to be only a few requirements for good care:

1. Chinchillas can tolerate cold, so don't keep them in too warm a room.
2. They need a dry climate, which is already present in our homes. So don't keep them in moist cellars, garages, or storage rooms.
3. They need a nutrient-poor diet containing ballast or roughage.

Life Cycle and Caging

These requirements are easy to fulfill and so chinchillas are particularly suited to be pets and will always be available in the future. The best way for the pet lover to keep them is doubtless as individuals "with family connections." Chinchillas need a place with as much quiet as possible to sleep during the day, so it's not good to select a busy hallway or a room into which street noises can penetrate. A quiet cellar, however, is not always suitable, for it's often too humid. When there is no other possibility, make sure there's at least enough fresh air and enough distance away from central heating vents or radiators. It's quite possible for the sudden crackling of an oil burner to startle a chinchilla out of its sleep, and then the animal won't calm down for a long time. Evenings, when our pets become alert, they crave activity and must be fed. Then they appreciate all the attention they can get from their owners. Don't go so far though, as to place their cages in the bedroom or children's room, for chinchillas jump around quite a bit during our sleeping time, leaping from a perch or platform down to the bottom of their cage, tossing the hay about and munching quite noisily on it. In the stillness of the night you can clearly hear their chisel-like teeth crushing into their feed. Then they'll carry up a food pellet, twig, morsel of dry bread or other hard object to their perch, where they'll either munch away on it or merely gnaw on any hard object just to wear their teeth down.

A female chinchilla (note the breeding collar) peering intently from her cage—maybe she spots food on the way!

Chinchillas are especially adapted to life in the high Andes and Cordilleras of South America. Nature has arranged for their breeding cycle to accommodate these natural conditions. The long winter is the best time for giving birth to the young, so fertilization occurs in the late autumn and the beginning of winter.

REPRODUCTION

Gestation lasts on the average for 111 days plus or minus three days, that is, it lasts almost four months. The young are born at the beginning of spring.

At this time of the year it can still be quite cold, so the mother has only one or two babies, which can be well provided for and kept warm. They are born fully furred, but they need their mother's help, for they have to solve a serious problem as soon as they enter the world. When the amniotic sac bursts, the babies are born soaking wet from the amniotic fluid. If their mother didn't help at once, there would be the danger that the newborn babies would stiffen in the cold. The mother wouldn't know how to help a stiffened, immobile baby, and she would simply let it die.

Luckily, the dry air, containing very little moisture, takes care of rapid drying. So the babies are immediately viable, see their mother, and follow along behind her for short distances. They keep in touch by emitting soft whistling sounds, answered by the mother's own whistle. The mother can feed the young for the first four weeks, but they also eat other foods after the first week. Luckily, the spring vegetation by this time has grown enough for the young to find sufficient food, and they feed themselves in about eight weeks. They grow up fast

FACING PAGE:
The young chinchilla shown with its hovering
mother isn't a newborn, but it's still young enough
to be given protection under her watchful eyes.

The newly born chinchilla shown here next to its mother will soon dry out and have its coat fluffed.

during the short summer and are ready to breed when winter starts, so the next generation can be born the following spring.

Naturally, in this harsh environment, only the animals who developed quickly and grew during the short time allotted will breed. Nature excludes weak females and underdeveloped males from breeding. They have to prove, during the harsh winter, whether they will be capable of reproducing the species. This severe natural selection and the small number of offspring are why wild chinchillas have always been scarce, thus making their fur very expensive, and why they were threatened with extinction by the fur trade's over-zealous hunting of them.

Even on breeding farms we can only partially overcome these natural obstacles, including the very low natural birth rate. For these reasons, for their size furs are still very expensive today, when hundreds of thousands of chinchillas are turned into fur coats yearly. We will always be limited here, for the natural limitation of the number of offspring cannot be overcome, and this problem will continue to give breeders headaches in the future, too.

Reproduction

Sexing

It is important for the pet owner to recognize his pet's sex. Males have proven to be best for caged life, and they are usually the ones being sold. Even the young animals can be told apart easily. Anus and urethra are close together in the female, separated only by a skin fold. In the males, the distance is further, and there is no skin fold.

These differences are even easier to see in older animals. To sex the animal (that is, tell its sex), take it out of the cage, grasp the base of the tail and lift it up. Looking at it from underneath, you can see how the anus and urethral outlet stand out a bit from the fur. Very little separation and a skin fold indicates a female. Separation of 5 to 10 mm and absence of skin fold means a male.

A mother beige chinchilla patiently waiting while her baby nurses.

CARE

First of all let it be said that our little rodents have a very pronounced sense of cleanliness and so are constantly cleaning themselves. So the creature itself doesn't need any care, although combing with a fine comb doesn't hurt and is even done with a hairdresser's perfection by breeders to dress up their animals at shows. Note, however, that the ordinary care of your pet does not require combing. Vermin haven't yet been found on chinchillas. Their thick fur is probably unsuitable for the development of fleas, mites, and lice. I've never heard any of my breeder colleagues complain about such pests, either.

The chinchilla's body odor is very slight and I believe is the least offensive for our noses, compared with mice, rabbits, rats, gerbils, chipmunks, guinea pigs and hamsters (in that order). Even droppings from healthy animals are odorless and don't soil the cage. Urine, however, when it decomposes, has an unpleasant smell. Luckily, chinchillas are very clean animals and pick out a permanent place in the cage to urinate, which you can service quite conveniently with litter once a week when you clean the cage.

Chinchilla hairs are somewhat of a problem. The hair is light and thin, so slight drafts can blow it out of the cage. Then you have to collect it, perhaps with a vacuum cleaner.

They are social animals and live in family groups. When we acquire one, we've got to take that fact into consideration. A chinchilla needs family contact. A single pet seeks this contact with his owner, who has to dedicate time to it. He's got to approach it quietly and confidently. When I come to the

FACING PAGE:
Upper photo: The teeth in an adult chinchilla normally have a yellowish cast, sometimes shading very slightly to reddish yellow, almost a very light orange. *Lower photo:* Scissors can be used to trim the hairs on the tail if they become ragged.

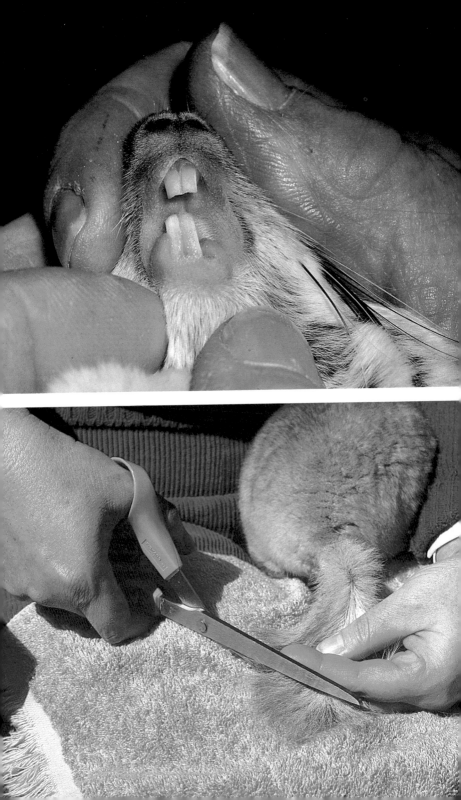

breeding room to feed them, the little rascals are already up against the wire. At other times, they disappear into the furthest corner of the cage, so they have a pronounced sense of time. Feeding should always be punctual, even when we're away on vacation; our pet sitter should be instructed to feed on time. Every time you come into the room, make vocal contact. They immediately recognize soft, friendly speech, and they usually respond with soft squeaking. Once this contact is established, a chinchilla will never take fright and dash around in the cage, possibly injuring itself, but will wait for its owner or

A chinchilla enjoying a dust bath. The walls of the receptacle used as the bathing place should be deep enough to prevent the dust from being scattered too much.

keeper, then rush at its food or snack as if he were almost starved to death. Always make these feedings, when at all possible, at the same time in the morning and evening. (see chapter on feeding for amount). A handful of good hay to supplement the feed is fine, too. Clean out and refill the water receptacle every evening. That is absolutely necessary to prevent soiling of the water container, thus avoiding intestinal infections. In addition to these absolutely necessary daily chores, there's the sand bath—very important for chinchilla cleanli-

ness—twice a week. In the wild, they "sand" bathe in the rock or mineral dust. Breeders can obtain similar products from the pet shop. Pet owners of single chinchillas only need some bird grit or gravel (1 cup) mixed with talcum (1 teaspoon). This mixture has similar properties and the same effect as natural dust or sand: it de-greases and cleans, keeping the chinchilla fur fluffy. Your pet will take a bath immediately once you provide a bowl containing this "dry bath" of dust, sand, or mixture of grit and talcum. You'll have to accept the miniature dust storm. Your chinchillas won't mind your watching, and, in fact, they couldn't put on a better show for you. A towel over the cage, however, might help keep the rest of the room sand-free during the "bathing."

Once a week remember to clean out the cage and replace the litter. Please don't use disinfectants all the time. It's sufficient to rinse the cage floor with plain water when the old

The use of disinfectants in either spray or liquid form shouldn't be depended upon as a regular part of cage maintenance, and no type of chemical preparation should ever be given to young children for application.

Pet shops carry many different types of litter materials that can be used in the chinchilla cage, so chinchilla owners have a wide variety to select from. Pet dealers can provide practical advice about the type of litter that will be best for your purposes.

litter or bedding material is removed, and then to dry it before adding fresh litter, sawdust or shavings. It's best to use coarse small animal litter which doesn't fly out of the cage so easily when the animals romp, and some absorbent litter in the corner where they are used to urinating.

Every six months, wash out the cage (without the chinchillas!) in the bathtub or shower and scrub it with a soft brush. And that's about everything you have to do for your pets. Along with all that cleaning, of course, don't forget to clean perches or platforms, short length of pipe (clay, etc., used for hiding), feed and water dishes, and the dry bathing bowl.

Always make sure the chinchillas are not kept in moist places. Many breeders have failed and many chinchillas have lost their lives because unscrupulous sellers have not explained the basic natural requirements for keeping this animal. Be sure to ventilate well in dry weather; don't worry about a little cold

weather, for our little pets are well protected by their fur. Cold can't hurt them; in fact, we think cold helps to form good fur. Dry, heated air is not harmful, either, but it should not be excessively warm. A room temperature of 68°F. (20 C.) is adequate.

Housing

The animals we buy all come from breeding establishments where they have been kept and bred for generations. Cages at those places are about 50 x 50 x 40 cm, so we can assume that size is tolerable for chinchillas. Only one animal should be kept in such a small cage. If several animals are kept together, then a larger cage is necessary. The cage should be large enough to provide many nooks or hiding spots. Chinchillas are not always friendly to each other. We have to allow for the male's fighting for his territory and for the times a female needs to escape from her mate. Following is a guide to the preparation and equipping of homemade as well as ready-made cages from the pet shop for housing chinchillas. Remember, chinchillas are rodents. That means that all cage parts must be of gnaw-proof material or heavy, resin-free wood which can resist sharp teeth for awhile.

Even though it's being observed at very close range, this chinchilla is not nervous, as it has become accustomed to sights and sounds associated with people.

1. One or two platforms halfway up. Chinchillas like to sit on the warm wood and also use the platform as a landing field when they leap around. Use strong boards at least 4½ to 5" (12 cm) wide. Replace them when they are gnawed up.
2. A clay or ceramic pipe about 4" (10 cm) in diameter and at least 12" (30 cm) long makes a good refuge (like a bear uses a hollow log!) for escaping disturbances. A little wooden box, too, is appreciated, but is soon chewed up.
3. For water, a rabbit drinker of glass is the easiest to keep clean. Open pans of water are soon soiled by the leaping chinchilla, and dirty water is often the cause of dangerous intestinal infections.
4. Dry feed can be given in an open stoneware dish stable enough not to be overturned by the romping animals and hard enough not to be gnawed to pieces.

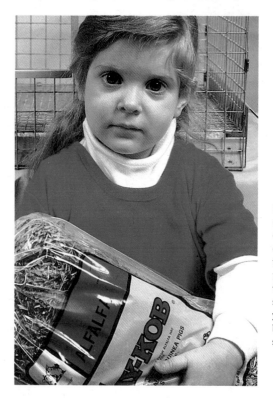

Hay has a number of different uses in connection with chinchillas. Make sure that you use a good packaged product of the type sold in pet shops; don't endanger your animals' welfare by using makeshift substitutes.

Care

5. Hay is very good fodder, best given in a hay rack so it doesn't lie on the cage floor, where it gets soiled.
6. A bath bowl of solid material must be in the cage. Chinchillas like to bathe. Because they originally come from a habitat where water is hardly available, they naturally bathe in a very particular way—they roll around in the dry rubble dust and powder their whole fur with it.

Every cage bottom should be provided with a deep pan of resistant plastic or galvanized tin. A litter layer of about 2″ (5 cm) is laid down and care taken that it doesn't become too displaced. But that's not enough to make your pets happy. They also need a tranquil spot to rest during the day (they are active mainly at dawn and twilight) and shouldn't be disturbed too often. The quietest place in your home is best. Homes are usually very dry these days and unfortunately lack humidity. Chinchillas, however, find that very tolerable. They would also appreciate not being too warm, if we can manage it.

Chinchillas must be provided with clean, fresh drinking water at all times. Notice that although the water reservoir portion of this drinking bottle is plastic, the spout is metal to prevent its being gnawed by the chinchillas.

Feeding and Diet

Breeders usually feed the whole stock morning and evening, which the pet owner should also do at home. The morning feeding should be light and conducive to the daytime rest period. The evening meal should provide energy for the nighttime activity.

Vitamin supplements can have a value in your chinchillas' dietary program, but don't rely on them to make up deficiencies in the regular feeding program.

The diet consist of four components:

Drinking water—Drinking water should be at room temperature and provided fresh daily. Fruit vinegar (1 teaspoon per ½ pint water) has been used successfully as a supplement to drinking water. For deficiencies, you can add Carlsbad salts (sodium sulfate plus sodium bicarbonate) as well as vitamins to the water.

Ready-made feed, pellet, etc.—Ready-made feed suffices for normal conditions. A good chinchilla feed is a proper diet, but so is rabbit food. A level tablespoon of feed is enough in the morning. For particularly exacting breeders or owners, here's a special feed for morning use: ⅓ coarse oats, ⅓ coarse wheat bran, ⅓ mixture of equal parts of linseed, yeast and dietary chalk or calcium.

Hay—Chinchillas, as creatures of arid regions of the high Andes, must eat parched plants and dry fruit remnants. For most of the year the dried-out plant life is especially important. That's why hay is so necessary for our pets. A handful of hay at each meal is a blessing for our little friend's diet. The hay

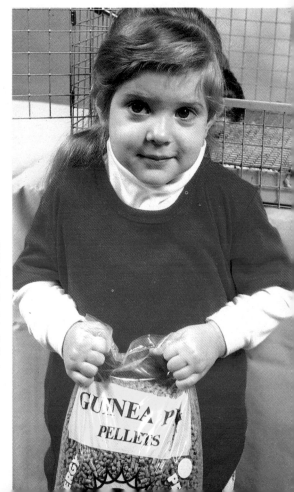

Although pellets designed for feeding to other small mammals such as guinea pigs and rabbits once were the only pellets available for chinchillas, they are now popular enough as pets to have their own pelleted foods obtainable at pet shops.

should be of the first harvest and coarse. Drying without any interruption by rain makes good hay. If it is well stored after that, at least half a year in a dry place, then we have a first-class hay which many breeders claim is alone adequate for feeding, especially in maturing the fur. Even the hay available at the pet shop is of this quality and can be used after testing it. It should always smell fresh and break upon bending. If no completely dry storage place is at hand, the hay can be dried out on the radiator.

Supplemental feed—Supplemental feed should be given only

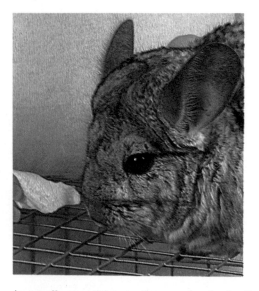

Greenfoods such as lettuce can upset the digestive system of a chinchilla if fed too often or in too great a quantity at one time.

in small quantities so these animals don't get used to an overly nutritious diet. Small amounts, however, are not bad for chinchillas and they help them get accustomed to your handling them. They like raisins best of all. It's better to buy the blue ones without sulfur (that is, no sulfur dioxide). The crackling of the paper bag is enough to unsettle our little pet. He hops back and forth and waits at the wire until you hand him a raisin, which he grasps between his front paws and gobbles up. Other dried fruits are good, too, such rose hips and dried thistle, a favorite delicacy. It's a good idea to pick a supply of these spiny flowers, wrap them together with string in bundles and store

Simulated bones available in pet shops can be offered to chinchillas, but not every chinchilla shows the same degree of appreciation of them.

them in a well-ventilated dry spot. It's amazing how the chinchilla will choose dried thistle over any other food or snacks.

Another foodstuff which you can store up yourself is tree branches—willow, hazelnut, fruit trees—all dried with bark and underlying cell layer (cortex or inner bark). These are good supplementary items in the diet and also serve as "teething" toys to sharpen gnawing teeth. Many animals prefer commercially available feed, simulated bones available at pet shops, and other supplementary diet items. Breeders often recommend dry bread, too, as a supplement, although be careful of the amount.

The same caution applies to greens. Some breeders praise them to the skies, others totally reject them. So the pet

owner must make his own choice. I've already supplemented the diet of my animals with small amounts of say, a dandelion leaf or narrow-leafed or broad-leafed plantain leaf apparently without doing them any harm. Just take care that any plants you collect are very fresh and not picked while still wet with morning dew. Also, avoid plants from near busy streets or highways; they may contain dangerous amounts of lead from fuel exhaust. Apples, too, have their just place. Give your chinchilla a small slice daily. Then there are the calcium preparations available on the market; various ones are used by breeders. They can also be used if your pet has a calcium deficiency. This is best seen in their teeth, which lose their white or brown coloration and become almost transparent. We've successfully tried half a tablet per animal daily.

Also, a gnawing stone to satisfy the urge to gnaw and sharpen the teeth is good, a pumice stone or a rabbit gnawing stone. In some cases, you can try a salt block for rodents, depending upon composition of the drinking water which makes more salt desirable. An indication that your pet craves salt is if it tries to lick your hands and arms when you play with it. In that case, you can make an exception and allow your chinchillas a few salt sticks, which they sometimes go wild about.

Dried carrots will not satisfy a chinchilla's urge to chew and have no value as objects on which it can gnaw and wear its teeth down.

Dried corn cobs broken down into small particles have started to find favor as a litter material for use in chinchilla cages.

DISEASES

Chinchillas are very disease-resistant animals when they are handled well and properly cared for. If, however, they don't seem as interested as usual at mealtime, and perhaps stay off in a corner, suspect some health problem. In this case, the droppings should be examined, for, besides the animal's change in behavior, the droppings are the best indication. Usually, the chinchilla runs around excitedly, leaving its droppings as it goes. If that does not occur, and if there are no droppings by morning, it might be a case of constipation, which has to be treated at once.

I am, in principle, against pharmaceutical products because nature has placed many remedies at our disposal which are quite adequate in such cases. In the case at hand, a teaspoonful of Carlsbad salts (see chapter on care) dissolved in a pint of water (to make a stock solution to add to the drinking water) has brought relief overnight. Constipation is caused chiefly by overfeeding, changes in location of feed, and the excitement associated with the changes. Timely recognition of the condition is essential for this treatment, so always observe the droppings of your pet. Later, the chances of a cure are slight because intestinal prolapse and intestinal occlusion may occur. Then, even a veterinarian can only rarely help. But don't let even intestinal occlusion discourage you. Several times I was successful in relaxing the intestine with a dropperful of cooking or salad oil, so it could be pushed back in. Following that, some good hay to eat and some of the stock solution of Carlsbad salts in the drinking water set things right again.

FACING PAGE:
An alert, keen-eyed expression is normal for a chinchilla. Check the eyes and general bearing of a pet chinchilla as an indication of its state of health.

The only form of constipation which may be antici- pated often occurs a few days before the birth of babies, and is caused when extreme dilation of the uterine horns (caused by a large litter of well developed babies being born) squeezes against the intestines. That corrects itself, however, at birth. By way of prevention, here too, Carlsbad salts in the drinking wa- ter can promote a good cleaning out of the intestines.

The main cause of all intestinal illness is nutritional dis- orders. Infections occur only rarely, but it is possible that chin- chillas with intestinal ailments can infect you. So in such cases, limit your contact with them as much as possible.

The nutritional status of the animal can be judged from its droppings. They should always be dry, about the size of a pea, and grayish black. Diarrheal symptoms start when droppings are not solid as usual, are wetter, and are soft enough so the animal squashes them on his perching platform. This can be taken care of by giving some good hay as ballast or roughage. Young animals get this easily because after birth they may be given too much feed. Reduction in the amount of feed and supplementation with hay is indicated in such cases.

When, despite these measures, the droppings do not get harder, there may be an intestinal ailment caused by spoiled feed. The only help in that case is to carefully examine the feed. Moist storage conditions can lead to fungus or mold growth on the feed or hay. Also, slime and algae may have grown in the water. Only self-evaluation of your procedures may help. Only when you are certain you haven't done any- thing wrong or anything you can't correct, should you have the veterinarian prescribe a medication; aureomycin and terramy- cin have had good effects.

The situation gets worse if the droppings are very soft and begin to smell unpleasant; then the veterinarian is the only one who can help; we can support his treatment by giving Carl- sbad salts, alternating with apple vinegar to promote healing and strengthen the chinchilla's resistance.*

* Be sure to let your vet know how you're supporting his treat- ment so there's no dangerous interaction with his pre- scriptions.

Diseases

Besides these intestinal conditions we've described, there's also what's called a chain dropping. It differs from diarrhea in that it consists of several small, about rice-grain sized fragments connected with hair-like threads. If you can see that, the ailment is already advanced. There might be improvement with a diet completely of hay and Carlsbad salts or fruit vinegar in the drinking water to bolster and reinforce resistance and self-healing forces. Animals which tend to have problems with their droppings, and which are weakened in other ways, should definitely receive this supplement in their drinking water. It won't hurt them and can increase their resistance and improve their total condition.

Less often, animals suffer from skin fungus which affects the smooth skin surfaces of the ears, feet and around the nose. That takes on a scaly look and doesn't shine anymore. Dandruffy bran-flake-like spots appear and begin to ooze, looking like scabies. For prevention, change the sand. Advanced

The chinchilla's paws are soft and padded.

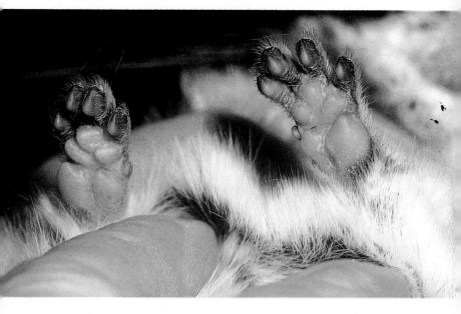

cases require the veterinarian to prescribe medication.

Besides these ailments, our pets, despite all our love for them, can suffer deficiencies, the most important of which I'd like to mention here. If your pet's white or light-brown incisors become almost transparent, a calcium imbalance may be the cause. See your pet dealer or veterinarian for medication.

Cramps occur only rarely in chinchillas, mainly in expectant females. An animal begins to feed, then suddenly it lies there and can't control its movement any longer, jerks convulsively, and breathes very rapidly. In a short while, it begins to crawl slowly; in about five minutes it runs around again quite normally and begins to feed. These are probably muscle cramps caused by rapid change from rest to activity.

Fur-Eating

Fur-eating or biting is one of the worst problems of chinchilla breeding. It's obvious that the goal of a breeder of fur animals is a perfect fur, otherwise he can't make a profit. For the pet lover, the situation is different. For him, the outside of the chinchilla is not as important as the whole pet and his total activity and happiness. Nevertheless, we've got to understand the situation in case it has to do with any nutritional or other errors in keeping our pet, which we can remedy.

The problem is quite easy to identify: the chinchillas exhibit irregularities in their fur. The fur is darker in some spots, and you can see that the tips of the hairs are bitten off or worn away. These places, too, look dark. Why does this happen? Housing many young animals in one cage can lead to the animals gnawing each other and fighting for food. Place the chinchillas in separate cages so the fur has a chance to fill out again, and after the fur grows back the chinchilla will look as good as a young furred one who was brought up alone. Fur-eating caused by external factors can still be treated to some degree. Perhaps your pet doesn't move around enough or is subjected to too much noise or disturbance to sleep during the day, which makes him nervous. Perhaps the room is too humid or otherwise not comfortable for the chinchilla. All of these external factors can unsettle your pet so much that it begins to chew on

Diseases

The patch of shorter fur shows signs of having been severely chewed down; the tips are missing completely.

its fur, making the furless spot larger and larger.

Improper dietary conditions, too, can cause fur-eating. Keep regular feeding times, stay with the usual food, and supply enough hay to occupy the animals longer than the other feed does. The results of this will soon tell you whether fur-biting was due to dietary problems. If it was, the chinchilla will return to its normally good looks.

Because fur-eating often occurs in young males not in-tended for breeding, as well as in receptive females, hormonal disturbances may be involved. But what can you do about it? There's no satisfactory answer yet. Is this problem hereditary? Many breeders say yes, others say no. No one has found a rem-edy. All things considered, one can observe the following: chin-

This chinchilla's body is being well supported as the animal is lifted through the opening to its cage.

chillas who feel comfortable with their owner and are well nourished and kept properly don't ever get this "disease." It is very difficult to help a heavily damaged animal. We've already had some success in treating some animals. Upon transfer of the affected animals to an open holding area, the condition cleared up in half a year in almost 60% of the animals. When they were transferred back to the breeding area, it started all over again.

Diseases

There has been a certain amount of success with "occupational therapy." The cage is filled with hay and straw, several willow, hazelnut or fruit tree twigs, and then the affected chinchilla is allowed to romp and rage around in it. You would be amazed to see how rapidly a chinchilla can expend energy. In one or two days all the hay or straw finally lies shredded up on the bottom of the cage and ignored. Then you've got to supply a new load, otherwise the treatment will not be successful. There are also many other possibilities. My best method is most amazing. Once the animal escapes and runs around the room, it gets only a pan of water. It's got to laboriously gather together its fellow chinchillas' feed pellets which fall out of the cage, and keep busy all night. In relatively short time, the condition of the fur improves. So is it perhaps really indeed the lack of movement and associated boredom which cause our animals to gnaw on their furs?

Many breeders have developed many remedies, many of which have been reported. Several of them are

(1) Valerian* drops in the drinking water have a calming effect, and have been successful in a few cases.
(2) Bacon rind or crackling hung in the cage to be gnawed on, certainly an effective cure here and there.
(3) Salt in water, or cattle saltlick block to be gnawed on (I'm successfully testing that now).

* Valerian plant parts, sold in health food shops, and brewed into a tea as a stock solution to add to the water, might be a substitute for drops—a European remedy.

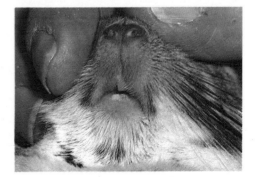

The nasal passages of a healthy chinchilla are normally entirely free of exudate.

Let's go back for a moment to the question of whether fur-eating can be hereditary. Breeders can certainly test and verify whether nervous disorders, unrest and lack of adaptability are inherited in certain breeding lines. My advice, then, is to pick out only calm animals with thick fur. The calm and phlegmatic ones of mine have never been fur-eaters. Perhaps this is useful advice for breeders, with whose help fur-eating can be eliminated or at least greatly reduced.

Judging from the literature available to me, I've found no one has yet studied whether this problem is perhaps hereditary in certain strains. I've found it much less common in the broad-heads (Costina type). This book cannot resolve the problem, but it can stimulate further research towards a solution.

Mummified birth product

I have often observed a small, grayish-black wad of hair and bone come out with the placenta following birth of chinchilla babies. This happened a few times with females who really should have been delivered much earlier. Close study has revealed that these females did not give birth to young the previous time; for some reason I did not know they died, and were

The light area on one side of the photo is normal fur; the dark area on the other side shows fur that has been chewed down, revealing the undercoat.

Chinchillas certainly aren't the most prolific of animals—but their babies are worth waiting for.

then completely resorbed into the mother's uterus. Only the bones and hairy fur were left over, similar to the little ball of left-over indigestible mouse fur and bone dropped by an owl. Then, after the next fertilization, which can proceed without complications, this indigestible residue is delivered along with the new litter. Until this new birth event, the chinchilla cannot eject the mummified bundle from the uterus; the exit passage is closed until the next heat period. Nevertheless, it is an amazing feat, which is still among the many other strange things we can observe in our chinchillas.

Hair ring in mature males

Chinchillas normally keep themselves very clean. The males, however, have a problem in which fine hairs can collect under the prepuce, which cut off the blood circulation and damage the penis. So, about four times a year check to see whether such foreign bodies have collected, and whether they can be removed with baby oil if need be. A male with a genital problem like this will sit with its legs pulled up.

Many pet lovers who have kept their pets successfully for a while would like to try breeding. Only if they can successfully breed their pets do they get the feeling that they have done everything right for their animals. That is naturally also true for chinchilla lovers, and is certainly especially appropriate for them.

PET OWNER TO BREEDER

Chinchillas are not easy to breed. They must be in good condition and feel comfortable in their surroundings; otherwise any attempts at breeding are doomed to failure from the start. Once you've gained the ability as a pet owner to understand the behavior of your pet and provide proper diet and housing, nothing hinders your trying your hand at breeding.

But please don't fall for the promises of unscrupulous sellers who offer to sell you expensive "breeding groups" and advice for a lot of money. My advice would be to first obtain a pair or one male and two females with which to make the first attempts at breeding. Try to obligate your supplier to buy the animals produced. You can make an arrangement of that type with some sellers, but unfortunately not very many.

Limit yourself at first to breeding animals which can be sold as pets, for that's still a good market in the future. You have to observe only the simplest rules and be able to recognize fur quality, including fur maturity, and be familiar with destroying the animals, skinning of the furs from them and selling them. Despite all of that, I still consider it important to continue your education by joining a group which promotes chinchilla

FACING PAGE:
Upper photo: A beige female and brown velvet male.
Lower photo: Two male chinchillas of "charcoal" color varieties.

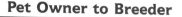

breeding. You can discuss problems with fellow members and get help from experienced breeders. To be sure, the main purpose of the these groups is chinchilla breeding for furs. But they all have to breed the animals first, and that's done all about the same way, so you have a mutual interest. You can learn how to judge chinchilla furs or the fur quality of living animals. Dues in the groups are not very expensive, so you can say that the expenditure is worth it. Also, the newsletters some clubs publish are quite informative.

Don't worry about all the talk about fur quality and similar things; improvement in quality is just the biggest problem at the moment. You should also not take it too tragically if your animals don't win first prize in the club's shows. Keep in mind that for pet lovers, the pet's whole being and personality is the reason we love them.

If, however, you're seized with ambition and fur quality does become your first commandment, then buy good animals from your breeder friends and slowly improve your stock. We should *not* do away with animals we've grown to love, which is often recommended so as to radically change our old stock to new. Our animals do not deserve being done away with. Many big breeders look back with misgivings and sadness to the time when all their animals had names and not just a number in a breeding record book.

Notice that the fur is considerably lighter in color on the underside of a chinchilla.

FACING PAGE:
Upper photo: This chinchilla exhibits good standard coloration and a fine-textured dense fur. *Lower photo:* This chinchilla enjoys being coddled and cuddled.

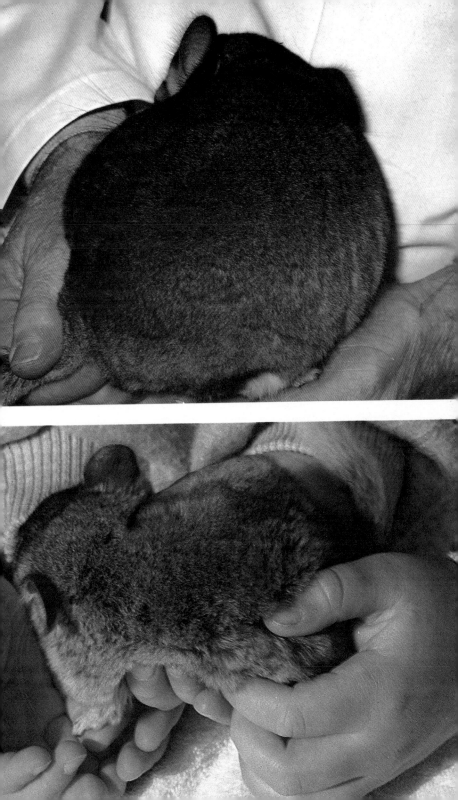

BIOLOGICAL INFORMATION

Chinchillas are rodents. The order Rodentia is represented all over the world, but the pet lover's knowledge about similar South American species is usually limited to the guinea pig. Only recently has the more unusual chinchilla caught on as a pet. The common feature of all chinchilla breeds is their characteristic unique hair color. Every hair has three color graduations. The lower part is dark gray, then comes a lighter band, and the tips are dark gray to black. This coloration is so typical that all animals with similar coat color are said to be chinchilla-color.

The fur consists of three zones, which can be easily distinguished: a dark back part which turns lighter gray to the sides, and then turns white on the underside of the body. The fur is very thick, and here nature has come up with something very strange. Many single, very thin, light hairs grow out of every hair root, providing for the fullness of the fur; up to 60 single hairs have been counted. To keep the coat resilient and silky, still other single hairs are built in—the guard or awn hairs. This hair structure makes the chinchilla first and foremost interesting as a fur provider.

The underlying skin is very thin, and the hairs are very loosely implanted. When a bird of prey seizes a chinchilla, this characteristic proves itself; if the bird doesn't strike firmly enough with its talons, it gets only a bunch of hair, and the chinchilla escapes with only a scary close call and damaged fur.

The ears are an indication of a very well developed sense of hearing, which helps the chinchilla to orient itself at

FACING PAGE:
This method of handling a chinchilla is definitely not recommended for the inexperienced; it is being used by a technician on a chinchilla ranch to give a full view of the pelt.

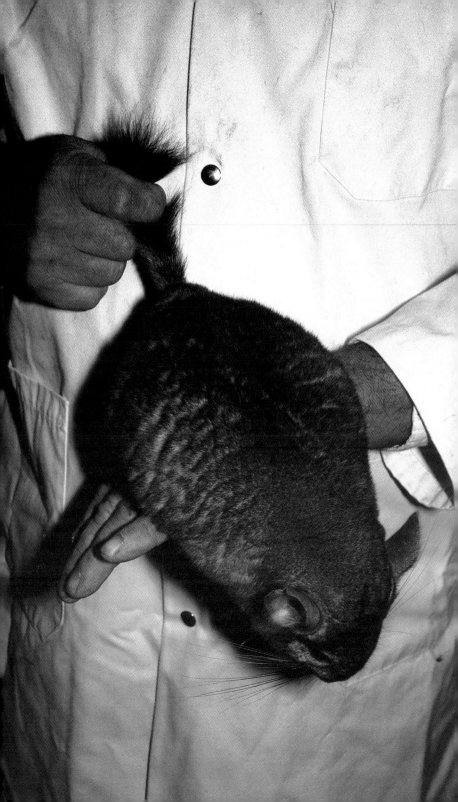

dusk or dawn. The tip of the snout is provided with a row of ever-moving feelers or sensitive whisker hairs which also help the animal to find its way around when it is active in darkened surroundings.

A chinchilla can use its forepaws almost as a squirrel does. It sits on its hind legs and nibbles off pieces of its food pellets. Its hind legs are more developed. That lets the animal flee swiftly, hopping away almost like a kangaroo. Its long bushy tail, which can attain about two-thirds of its total body length, is used as a support for sitting, and is covered with bristle or whisker hairs; it can be used as a "handle" if you've got to quickly and firmly grasp the animal.

Chinchillas are mature for breeding at about eight months of age. They have a gestation period of 111 days, which can vary slightly one way or the other. The main mating period occurs in late autumn, so that the young can be born at the end of winter or beginning of spring. To protect the female, nature has provided a very effective device. The entrance to the vagina is closed almost all year, and open only in receptive females, ejecting a wad or plug. This plug of mucoid secretions is a signal to the male that the female is ready for mating. That's not always so easily done, however, for many females want to be wooed first. When mating has occurred, the male's ejaculate and the female's vaginal secretions form a plug, which indicates to the breeder that fertilization has taken place. This allows him to record the precise birth date. Day of mating + 111 days = day birth is expected.

Chinchilla females have a special kind of double uterus, each side used alternately for giving birth to the young, and then recuperating. This is important because after giving birth, the female remains "open" and any other fertilization at that time occurs in the other side, letting the recently used one rest.

Only very strong females should be permitted this fertilization shortly after giving birth; the male may have to be kept away until the next time, so that the female can busy herself with her litter.

At first, she must clean up and lick her young dry. This does not present any problem when, as is normally the case,

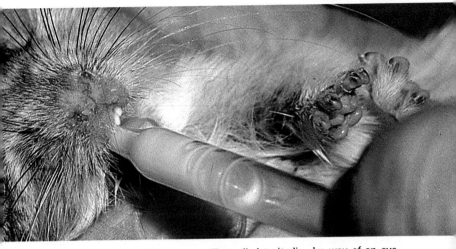

A newborn baby chinchilla having milk applied to its lips by way of an eye-dropper.

only one or two babies are born; in multiple births, however, the pet owner has to help by keeping some of the babies warm in a woollen cloth until the mother finishes with expulsion of the placenta. Otherwise babies stiffen with cold and die. When the mother has eaten the placenta, dried off the first baby and has it crawl under her to keep warm, that's the time to place the next baby in the cage, and so on until all the litter mates have been taken care of.

Soon the newborn search through their mother's fur for her teats. If no more than two babies are there, then this nourishment is fully sufficient. If the milk is not enough when multiple births occur, then the mother doesn't like to let her young get to her teats any more. If you examine her, you can often see bite wounds; the young bite furiously at her teats when the milk runs out. The only help here is feeding supplemental milk, which you can find in pet shops as breeding milk for dogs or cats. It's prepared according to the instructions and dripped with a small dropper onto the snout. The young animal begins at once to lick these drops, which can be given until the youngster has had enough. Doing this in the morning and evening allows the mother's teats to recuperate.

Clipping of the teeth and filing down of the stumps is recommended in this case, but a lot of skill is needed so that the operation does not damage the tooth bed and so that the price of this temporary help is not permanent damage.

The substitute feeding with the milk mentioned above is to be carried out well enough so as to care also for orphans who have lost their mother. It's best, however, to first try a foster mother who perhaps has her own baby of the same size to feed. Try it in any case, even if there's the risk that the would-be foster mother rejects the youngster.

If artificial rearing is the only possibility, then fresh milk has to be mixed up every two hours and given in the necessary quantities from 6 a.m. to 10 p.m. Also, warm housing is necessary. Place a sufficiently large wooden crate with a wire-screen cover near the heater in such a way that the wood is just warm to the touch. In about a week, the young start to eat alone from their mother's feed. This goes for those fed artificially, too.

In six to eight weeks, the youngsters are separated from their mother. It's best not to take all away at once. Every three days take one and put it in an individual cage so that its

Viewed from the side, the incisors are seen to be chisel-shaped, but they should be level and regular in outline.

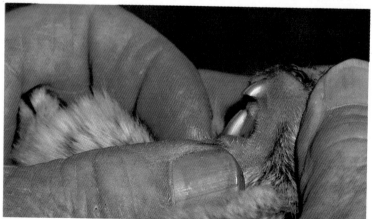

The dust bath should be a regular part of a pet chinchilla's grooming regimen.

fur can develop well. The mother is unburdened, and the growth of smaller youngsters can be encouraged with extra food. The mother's milk production can then be reduced so as to avoid engorged teats or milk glands, which can lead to inflammation.

Weaning the young is a difficult time in the life of the little ones. The greatest mistake which can be made here is overfeeding, which can lead to thin droppings and diarrhea. So keep in mind that feed quantity should only be half as large as for breeding animals.

It is important to mention that the young absolutely must be housed in individual cages; otherwise they would injure themselves with the scuffling around for food and playing roughhouse, damaging their coats. The young chinchillas should have their sandbaths daily so that their fur develops well. In addition, take care that perching platforms and cage bottoms are kept scrupulously clean, because discoloration of their fur with droppings or urine cannot be removed, and makes the fur practically useless. Also, it's very difficult to judge the quality of the fur and decide which animals are to be kept for breeding and which are to be skinned. The first time

Its eyes are open, but this newborn baby chinchilla is still rather bedraggled.

you make this kind of decision, get advice from professionals and don't act on your own. This first decision should be when the stock is about eight months old, because then the fur is approximately mature and it's easiest to decide.

In judging which animals are to be kept and bred, their ancestry as well as their appearance is important. Always try to improve a strain by using the young of parents who have already demonstrated good breeding characteristics, and by eliminating problem animals from breeding. That involves accurate record keeping and effective marking of the animals. Tattooing is available, but to me the better way seems to be small ear clamps, which are easily attached and permit close control. Every young animal at my place is immediately written up on a filing card, with age group, serial number, sex and birthdate; the serial number is attached to the cage to facilitate supervision and avoid mix-ups. Upon weaning the cage identification is transferred to the rearing cage. When the young are evaluated, those suitable for breeding are identified with ear markings. In addition, the animal's ancestry is noted on the card. The genealogical tree of the whole group can play a decisive role. On each animal's filing card are noted all items of personal information, and thus can be quickly referred to when evaluating animals. When new breeding groups are assembled, the

Biological Information

male and female cards provide a total picture for study.

In general, the usual breeding method is polygamous mating. The earlier method of mating pairs is not so common now because of the cost of feeding the many males. The modern way consists of a row of individual cages, each containing a female. A common corridor connecting all these cages gives the male access to all females except when a sliding or hinged portion closes off a female's cage to give her some respite from the male. To keep the females from leaving their cages, they wear a tin or plastic collar which does not pass through the doorway, which, however, is large enough to admit the male. In case the female is not receptive and grows aggressive, the male can quickly retreat and wait for a better time.

When assembling a new breeding group, it's best to leave one cage unoccupied so the male can be fed extra rations; sometimes he also eats with the females. During the breaking-in phase, small hiding spots can be built in here and

Closeup of an infant chinchilla. The ears have not yet attained their characteristically rounded and erect appearance.

there to let the animals have some privacy.

Breeding groups are variously composed, 4 to 20 animals being the usual number. This method has rapidly led to improved breeding strains during recent years, because with just one first-class male a large number of offspring can be bred and transmission of hereditary factors easily accomplished. Breeding on a large scale requires concern with genetics, and there are many books on the subject.

Mutations

Today the term *mutation* includes all changes and disruptions in the genes (carriers of inheritance). It covers changes which appear suddenly and can be inherited. In nature, certain mutations do not survive (such as coloration which is too obvious to predators). In breeding, however, mutations are often the basis of the selection of new colors or other varieties.

The first reported mutation in chinchillas was a white male born April 21, 1955 in America on Wilson's farm. Another mutation, now already quite widespread, is the so-called black velvet, in which the back and face are velvety black. This coloration is a favorite among hobbyists because it looks so smooth and is already available to a small extent on the pet market. Besides these mutations, there are many more, and we can almost say that every year brings new ones. Here is a list of the best known colors:

Light and dark sapphire	Blue velvet
Light and dark beige	Velvet
Silver	Light and dark brown
Blond	Charcoal
Pastel	Violet

Many breeders are ambitiously eyeing the prospects of breeding as many kinds as possible. That is inadvisable and would split up the industry too much. A limited choice must be made so as to avoid overuse of available breeding space, which makes good breeding results impossible.

The following books by T.F.H. Publications are available at pet shops and book stores everywhere.

CHINCHILLAS AS A PROFITABLE HOBBY— By Gerhard Schreiber
PS-852
Hardcover, 5½ × 8½"
160 pages, 65 photos

SUGGESTED READING

As Author Gerhard Schreiber points out in this detailed, explicit round-up of good advice and highly practical recommendations, breeding chinchillas requires patience, persistence, and perseverance. It also of course requires a good deal of knowledge, and this book—based on the observations and research of author Schreiber and other successful European breeders—provides that knowledge. Generously illustrated, including many attractive full-color photos.

DISEASES OF CHINCHILLAS—By Professor Dr. Helmut Kraft
PS-851; Hardcover, 6 × 9"; 144 pages
Contains more than 20 full-color photos

This book is considered the best available in Germany, where chinchillas are raised by thousands of hobbyists. The book is written for the serious chinchilla hobbyist, dealer and breeder, and it's so good that it can even be helpful to vets.

BREEDING AND CARING FOR CHINCHILLAS—By Egon Mösslacher
PS-850; ISBN 0-86622-118-2
Hardcover, 5½ × 8½"; 128 pages
Over 40 full-color photos

This book has been designed to be of special value to all of the many new chinchilla owners looking for good information about their pets; it provides all of the information they need to allow them to enjoy their pets to the fullest PLUS valuable sections dealing with the breeding of chinchillas.

ALL ABOUT CHINCHILLAS—By Karen Zeinert

PS-845; ISBN 0-86622-143-3
Hardcover, 128 pages, 5½ x 8"
49 full-color photos, 7 black and white photos

ALL ABOUT CHINCHILLAS presents the "soup to nuts" of chinchilla care in an easy-to-read format garnished with nearly 50 full-color photos. Written by a recognized expert in chinchilla culture and care, the book provides a wealth of concise, no-nonsense advice.

CHINCHILLA HANDBOOK—By Edmund Bickel

PS-853
Hardcover, 5½ x 8"
224 pages, over 40 full-color photos

Probably no one in the world had as much practical experience with chinchillas as the author of this book. His contributions to the art and science of chinchilla management and breeding are enormous. Now English-speaking chinchilla fanciers and breeders have a chance to benefit from Edmund Bickel's vast experience as well, because this book (generously illustrated with full-color photos) is the distillation of over half a century of his experiences with and observations of chinchillas from every commercial standpoint.